THE PEMMICAN EATERS

POEMS

MARILYN DUMONT

ECW Press | a misFit book

"What the map cuts up
the story cuts across."

— Michel de Certeau,
The Practice of Everyday Life

ACKNOWLEDGEMENTS

I gratefully acknowledge the Canada Council for the Arts,
Edmonton Public Library Writer in Residence Program as well as
Brandon University's Aboriginal Writer in Residence Program for
the creative time to produce these poems.

Earlier versions of some of these poems have appeared in the
following periodicals and anthologies: *Exile, Legacy, West Coast Line,
Prairie Fire,* and *Alberta Views.*

"Letter to Sir John A. Macdonald" was previously published in
A Really Good Brown Girl, Brick Books, 1996.

In memory of my brothers,
William James Vaness, Ambrose Danny John Dumont,
and my father, Joseph Ambrose Dumont.

Contents

Our Gabriel

In the late '60s, several members of my family dared to speculate we might be related to Gabriel Dumont, Louis Riel's general in the 1885 Riel Rebellion. I was ten years old and it was the first time I had heard of such an historical figure. My father showed only mild interest in the portrait of Gabriel on the thin paperback that my eldest brother held in front of him: *Gabriel Dumont, Indian Fighter* by Sandra Lynn McKee. It was the type of popular history book sold in gas stations and little gift shops along the Trans-Canada Highway, displayed with other provocative titles like *Murder on the Plains* or *The Lost Lemon Mine.* I remember thinking it highly unlikely that we could have descended from a figure important enough to have a book written about him. There seemed to be nothing remarkable about our family lineage. We were a large, poor Métis family living in small-town Alberta, having migrated from the north-central part of the province so that my father could find work. I assumed that if we were related, it was so distant all we could share was a last name.

My family had just relocated to Golden, British Columbia. Lured there by better wages in the booming BC logging industry, an industry in which he and mother had eked out an existence for twenty years near Sundre, Alberta. My father logged lodge pole pine and my mother was a camp cook. It was a no-frills life, supporting nine children on a faller's and camp cook's wages. Our house in Sundre was an old one-room schoolhouse. My parents worked away from home, in a logging camp during the week, while my older brother and sister cared for another brother and me. My father hunted moose and deer to keep meat on our table. Friday evenings my parents came home via the grocery store, with other essentials like fruit and vegetables. My mother supplemented any store-bought bread with large slabs of baked bannock.

Our home was frequently a halfway house for men from the Kikino Métis Settlement who sought work in the bush with my

1

father. My parents had moved off the settlement in the early 1940s, not long after the Alberta Métis Population Betterment Act established a land base for the destitute Métis population. Many Métis lived on road allowances and survived on what they could hunt or trap. Even though moving from the settlement meant leaving relatives and a Cree-speaking community, relocation to a small non-Native rural community held more promise with a school, public services, and hope of gainful employment. (Today, most, if not all, Métis settlements boast schools and local businesses.)

In Golden, we rented a tiny two-bedroom trailer with an extra room built onto one side. That space accommodated my parents, my two older brothers, and me, the youngest of nine children. When my married brothers and sisters and their families visited, this tiny trailer burgeoned with bodies.

One of the brothers who visited from Alberta had married a woman who was very interested in Canadian history and the Riel "resistance" period. I'm not sure if we knew at the time where her interest originated, or even if she knew, but years later when her genealogical research revealed that she was descended from Major-General Middleton (who commanded the Canadian troops against Riel), the irony was not lost on us.

Throughout those years, we began to collect books on Gabriel Dumont, Louis Riel, Métis history, and the rebellion. Apparently, the publishing world knew others were interested in this history too, particularly in Dumont. In 1975 Hurtig Publishers released *Gabriel Dumont* by George Woodcock, which ignited the imagination of Canadians about Dumont, whose influence in the Métis rebellions had previously been overshadowed by the controversial Louis Riel.

I recall studying these books and scrutinizing the photographs of Dumont, as if the keys to unlocking our family history lay somewhere in the sepia. Sandra Lynn McKee's biography of Dumont, the thin newsprint paperback, bore a black-and-white photograph of Dumont on the cover that slightly horrified me.

His balding head, rugged face, ratty beard and buffalo-hair lined vest so dominated his chest, it appeared he had a bald crown, but unusually long and bushy braids flowing down his barrel chest. His eyes were intense and disarming. I saw no resemblance between him and my father. However, in another black-and-white photograph of Gabriel posing in a suit, I did see a resemblance. Their facial features had a striking similarity: a square face; defined broad nose; and wide, flattened bottom lip. As I examined full body shots of the broad-shouldered, stout Dumont, I saw an uncanny likeness between him and my father.

I don't think my father or any of us knew how much family pride would stem from recovering the knowledge of our lineage, but I do remember my father's posture straightening and his face lighting up as more of his children showed interest in our connection to Gabriel Dumont. And the time for recovering this family history was ripe. It was the late 1960s, the era of protests against the Vietnam War, of women's and civil rights marches, the publication of Maria Campbell's memoir *Halfbreed*, the standoff at Wounded Knee, and Canadian Aboriginal leaders Harold Cardinal and Stan Daniels capturing media attention. The opportunity for recovering our Aboriginal ancestry could not have been better.

Perhaps it was a relief to my father to believe that he came from such noble beginnings despite his own father's loss of a homestead situated on land that lacked sufficient water to support a farm. I'm sure he was bemused by his children's sudden interest and even more puzzled by the capricious nature of public opinion about Aboriginal culture and history. With these changing times our history could be reclaimed, and my father's past wasn't merely the story of poor, struggling halfbreeds, but of a proud descendant of Gabriel Dumont, Riel's general.

As my family collected more books on Métis history, one of my older brothers researched the Dumont crest (of French origin) and proudly showed it to the rest of us. We joined provincial Métis organizations and became aware of Métis events, such as Back to Batoche Days in Saskatchewan. My mother bought a subscription to *New Breed* magazine. My nieces and nephews, when studying Canadian history in their classrooms, were acknowledged because of their link with the Dumont name. One of my nieces was named Gabrielle. Just saying our name in public summoned pride in us.

I don't know if there was a pivotal moment for me as much as it was a lengthy process of historical enquiry and gradual acceptance. We had no genealogical record, and I admit that, without it, I doubted our ancestry for years.

Then the genealogical record came to me. I was an undergraduate at the University of Alberta, when the late Dr. John Foster, a history professor, offered me a copy of six church-ledger-size pages that traced the Dumont genealogy back to Jean Dumont and his three sons: Gabriel (senior), Isadore, and Jean. Isadore fathered the famous Gabriel Dumont. Our family descended from Gabriel Senior who lived in the Edmonton area and was captain of the hunt at Lac Ste. Anne.

Upon discovery that *our Gabriel*, Gabriel Dumont Senior, our great-great-grandfather and uncle of the famous Gabriel, had held the position of leader at Lac Ste. Anne, I finally understood why our family's annual summer visit to the pilgrimage was so important to us. In 1842 Gabriel Senior guided the Oblate missionaries and Abbe Thibault to Lac Ste. Anne when it was established as a mission and Métis settlement. And it was Abbe Thibault who sanctified the *marriage du pays* of the elder Gabriel Dumont.

We referred to the pilgrimage as *the Lake*. My parents and eight siblings and I piled into a half-ton truck and drove 400 kilometres from Sundre to Edmonton and then another eighty kilometres northwest of Edmonton where, yearly, 30,000 or more Aboriginal people attended the Lac Ste. Anne Pilgrimage. It was the longest yearly trip we made. For the journey my father constructed a canvas canopy over the back of the truck bed. It looked a little like a chuck wagon, and this is where my siblings, ranging in age from seven to sixteen, rode along with our tents, tarps, tools, grub box, sleeping bags, camping gear, and clothes, while I, the youngest, rode in the cab with mom and dad.

My parents had been going to the lake as long as they could remember. If my father ever knew his original family connection to the lake, he never spoke of it, but it is certain that the site was steeped in our family's past. Perhaps my father wasn't even conscious of why Lac Ste. Anne meant so much, and maybe this is what happens to memory when ritual takes its place.

The Lac Ste. Anne Pilgrimage is one of the foundations of my cultural memory. It is where my parents taught me to remember our relatives through prayer after their passing. Invoking their memory through the place, people, and ritual was a way of affirming ourselves. For a large family with few economic resources, not unlike most of the families there, the affirmation of belonging — spiritually and ancestrally — was what sustained my parents through their physically demanding work and uneasy life in a southern Alberta town where Aboriginals were a disdained minority.

My family's acknowledgement of our blood connection to Gabriel Dumont has taken a long time. I frequently found my lack of interest in history puzzling, fraught with a reluctance to approach a subject that seemed merely to recount the lives of famous men; I knew the history of women, like my mother, deserved retelling too. Perhaps this loyalty to my mother was part of the reason for not writing about Gabriel Dumont before now.

Otipemisiwak

maybe Poundmaker
or even Big Bear
would have dreamt
those waking figures
Gatlin gun sorrows
bullets, crosses and misguided soldiers
if they were Riel
or Dumont
while Macdonald
swilling spirits
was in some crystal case of glory

and Louis dreamt
that supposedly
in broad daylight
the dawn
on its unseen bone
was lifting
above the fire

I don't believe
he was merely mistaken
regardless of
how little daylight remained

this evening
I retrieved a piece of birch bark
and something more
like a petrified limb
lay in the palm of a snowdrift

I thought of Louis
the way he kept envisioning
what was inside the dimness

how he dreamt of it ascending
on its unseen limb
how he wanted it to reflect
like water

Otipemisiwak: the Free People

LETTER TO SIR JOHN A. MACDONALD

Dear John: I'm still here
and halfbreed,
after all these years
you're dead, funny thing,
that railway you wanted so badly,
there was talk a year ago
of shutting it down
and part of it was shut down,
the dayliner at least,
"from sea to shining sea,"
and you know, John,
after all that shuffling us around to suit the settlers,
we're still here and . . .

We're still here
after Meech Lake and
one no-good-for-nothin-Indian
holdin-up-the-train,
stalling the "Cabin syllables / Nouns of settlement,
/ . . . steel syntax [and] / The long sentence of its exploitation"[1]
and John, that goddamned railroad never made this a great nation,
cause the railway shut down
and this country is still quarreling over unity,
and Riel is dead
but he just keeps coming back
in all the Bill Wilsons yet to speak out of turn or favour
because you know as well as I
that we were railroaded
by some steel tracks that didn't last
and some settlers who wouldn't settle
and it's funny we're still here and callin ourselves halfbreed.

Notre Frères

We were born beneath the water
in the darkest depths of the lake
We rise, our hooves rumbling
spewing lake water, muzzles dripping

in the darkest depths of the lake
Will Gabriel call, us, his brothers
spewing lake water, muzzles dripping
pulling the universe in our sway

Will Gabriel call, us, his brothers
riding his swiftest buffalo runner
aiming Le Petit
pulling the universe in their sway
the Milky Way — dust of buffalo spirits passing

Riding his swiftest buffalo runner
Will Gabriel, aiming Le Petit
rise, his horse's hooves rumbling?
dust of buffalo spirits passing

We were born beneath the water

LI BUFLOO

we came from the buffalo wallows
bowls in the earth hollowed out —
by the backbones of our greater ones
those who have returned now,
through those same curves in the earth

we are ghosts now, but once were
after the Dog days
after the Dog days, the horse and the gun

came our children
speaking our language
the same language as water
the same language as grass

we cradle buffalo rocks
our children, now
waiting

when will Gabriel call us back?
when will he put his ear to the ground
to find us once again?

when will Gabriel call us out?
our great heads swiping side to side
pulling the universe in our sway
the Milky Way twisting in our horns
shaking bright burning dust
to earth

How to Make Pemmican

Kill one 1800 lb. buffalo
Gut it
Skin it
Butcher it
Slice the meat in long strips for drying
Construct drying tripods and racks for 1000 lbs. of wet meat
Dry it while staving off predators for days
Strip from drying racks and lay on tarps for pounding
Pound 1000 lbs. of dry meat
Mix with several pounds of dried berries, picked previously
Add rendered suet

Cut buffalo hides in quarters
Fill with hot dried meat, berry and suet mixture
Sew quarter-hide portions together with sinew
Bury in a cache for later   mmmh.

I WANTED TO TREAT THEM AS WE
WOULD HAVE TREATED BUFFALO

"I wanted to treat them as we would have treated buffalo."[3]
— Gabriel Dumont of Middleton's men

When you said of Middleton's men, you wanted to treat them as buffalo,

was it because you had the fastest buffalo runner and steadiest shot?

Was it because you knew you could ride a buffalo runner, its neck
outstretched in full gallop on the heels of a herd holding the muzzle
loader upright till the last second to drop a wet slug down the barrel,
thrusting your gun forward to dislodge the shot while pulling the
trigger all at the same time,

you knew alone on the prairie, you could make a shelter and clothing
from their hides and food from their flesh and tools from their bones,
you knew the vibration of their hooves riding in the midst of them, the
feel of their hides — dry and coarse, you knew their snorting, the stone
weight of their bodies, their bulging terror-struck eyes, the taste of their
marrow, their sweet smoked jerky

Did the hunter in you imagine these men predictable as les animaux

Did the buffalo caller imagine predicting the direction of their advance

Did you imagine their heads heavy with thoughts of dividing the land
for their use alone

Did you believe they like the buffalo would eventually disappear into
holes in the earth?

Les Animaux

"This summer I planted ten acres in potatoes and barley.
The ferry gave me more work than I wanted. We lived pretty
good without the hunting. In 1880 or 1881, I led the last
Saskatchewan hunts, but les animaux were gone and out ancient
ways went with them. "[4]
— Jordan Zinovich, *Gabriel Dumont in Paris*

gone, uncle they're gone

and something in us goes too following after

les animaux, those who you "called" as if they were your brother

les animaux, those who you called mon frère and herded with their
great beards

les animaux, the brothers that have left us   they have moved
to another plain,

uncle, on the last hunt instead of seeing a moving sea of brown
backs, a rippling

ground

now, you see only a few stumps   feeding on grasses

now, their great size is swallowed by the bigger prairie

prairie, that once seemed like it couldn't hold all

les animaux, their sound like distant thunder   will never reach
your ears again

uncle, how sad that day   when no one spoke of them

as if speaking their name

could slice an arm from one's own body

because they were you

     were you less of a man because of them?

les animaux made you captain of the hunt

now, you are the captain of fighting men standing ground

against the settlers rolling in by the thousands

now, *they* are the new herds,

but they're not les animaux

the brothers that fed and clothed us

and gave us reason to dance

gone, and now the prairie is mute

Michif problem family among the nuclear language types   one
parent French   the other Cree/Salteaux   wintering words:
sliced thin, smoke-dried, pounded fine, folded in fat and berries
pemmican not pidgin or creole   combining two grammatical
maps   paddle trade routes along waterways   traverse
rapids: white and dangerous with Ojibway women à la façon du
pays   Métis traders, speak la lawng of double genetic origin
pleasure doubled   twice the language   twice the culture
         mixta, not mixed-up, nor muddled   but completely
FrenchCreeOjibway   different tongues   buffalo, a
delicacy source language right from the cow's mouth   mother
of all in-group conversation   wintering camps dispersal
neither Cree, Salteaux nor French exactly, but something else
not less   not half   not lacking

What we don't need

An expert, in the audience asks why we didn't invite a linguist
    to our Michif & endangered languages panel

    It's because what we don't need is another expert,
another expert   to inform us our direct action on human rights was
a rebellion

another expert to perpetuate a belief that our Michif language
    is either poor Cree or broken French

another expert to teach us how to be farmers at St. Paul-des-Métis
or Red River
    when "our failures" were the state's misguided pilot projects in
civilization,

another expert to deny that our Creation stories — momentous
    when the Clovis theory slowly crumbles under our small, small
stories,

another expert to sell us script as our homeland
    when most of it was speculated and today, we have no homeland
at all

another expert to tell us our spiritual beliefs are "heathen"
    when what this planet needs is Earth-centred beliefs

    no, what we don't need is
another expert who can be bought by industry and government
                         to lead us to our own destruction

October 1869: to smoke their pipes and sing their songs

Louis planted his beaded moccasin on the survey chain
cutting across André Nault's river lot
pitched there by men
slung with transits, levels, and measuring sticks
men looking to the horizon
calculating the *free land* for homesteaders

"You go no further," commanded Louis

blocking their line of sight
their ledger of lines
angles, meridians, and parallels
corrections for curvature
iron stakes at the corners
of perfect square miles

although over fifty million acres
was surveyed
made ready
ready-made
for occupation

there were no quarter sections
for "the miserable halfbreeds,"[6]
"the pemmican-eaters"[7]

but any man over eighteen
with a vacant quarter in the NWT
homesteaded

did the survey record in its calculations
witness whose lives were fragmented by these precise
coordinates?

could their instruments
determine the number of years
Nault had lived and cleared brush
harvested firewood on the same land he was now barred from?

did the surveyor's coordinates record the number of letters, the
number of signed petitions

did it detect the colourless voices of the Settlers' Rights Association
joining in Louis' protest

did their instruments detect their words plain as bread "we have not
been consulted in any way as a people entering into the Dominion"[8]

where did this penchant for measuring and marking derive?

this desire to count and delineate this land
account for it

rename and grip it
like shovels, axes, and saws
lug like trunks,
steer like plows
pile like lumber

where did this taste for counting begin
its long rooted self
calculating angles and slopes
long conjuring "empty" land into property
the long root of capitalism
boring mineral veins
drilling wells
forcing steam down bored holes
extracting dark thick fluids
stabbing the land-belly
sucking every seam
and filling the gaping holes with
with the toxic unseen

I am told   when I survey from the top of a hill
I take into account the entire land
upon which I stand;

I count this place

what conjuring does the mind do
measuring a hill,
the angle of its slope,
is it easier to climb?

is it in the imagined embrace of mother?
minds hover
oversee her

capture, hold

I take into account this entire land

land, upon which I stand

I count this place

I count this space my own

when two lines cross, the saleable land is multiplied by two
the survey lines that scored this land were
so it could be ripped along its edges, cliffs, and deeper memories

Lines

these are not the lines of the steeple at Batoche
or the wheel runnels of Red River carts scoring the prairie
or the lines of women and children following after
or the threads of their L'Assomption sash

these are not survey lines severing river lots into acres, quarters, sections
these are not the bloodlines of mixed marriages
nor the rail lines of the Iron Horse
nor the lines of Middleton's men marching in red serge
these are not the lines of prairie fire confusing the troops
nor the gun trenches dug deep near St. Antoine de Padua
nor the reins held tight by Gabriel
crossing the Medicine Line

these are not the lines of the cross held by Riel in battle
or his lines of testimony in a Regina courtroom
these are not the lines of Métis being sentenced for treason
the lines of a foreign law they transgressed
or the worry lines of their women praying
or the lines of hymns they sung in Cree

these are not the lines between English and French
these are not the lines between oral and written history
these are not the lines of the rope that hung Louis

NOT A SINGLE BLADE

"You are looking for Gabriel? Ah! You are wasting your time.
There is not a single blade of grass on the prairie that he does not
know!"
— Father Alexis Andre, Oblate of Mary Immaculate, who
accompanied Riel to the scaffold in 1885[9]

Not a single blade

of grass on the prairie

you do not know

not a single blade

will betray and

reveal your whereabouts

After the arrival of Middleton, the North West Field Force, and the
Gatling gun

after the death of your uncle, Aicawpow, in battle

after the troops set fire to your house and stable

after they confiscate your prized herd of horses and your billiard
table

after Madeleine and Louis hide in the trees

after you are shot and wounded in the head

you will not surrender

instead you gather eighty rifle and forty revolver cartridges and firearms

from the Métis who surrendered or died

from the Canadian forces lying dead in the field

you will not be taken alive

and not a single blade

of grass will renounce you

your life depending on the coulees, leaves, limbs, and blades of buffalo grass

So for four days at dawn, you follow Les Anglais' patrols searching Batoche

as morning light glints off their gun barrels

and their horses' breath signaling the direction of their advance

you trail them, riding in their tracks to avoid being tracked hiding in the bluffs

concealed in the coulees

crouched in the willows

the May nights cold along the river

Invisible but hunted

you slipped through their sight

to become the dogwood lining the South Saskatchewan

the ascending light at dawn and descending light at night

the poplars and cottonwoods flourishing along the river

the force of fierce winds pushing the soldiers back

the dust blown in their faces

When they moved, you moved

they stopped, you stopped

and each night you'd return to Batoche for refuge

until the next morning, you'd wait

watch them saddle-up

and set out again in their tracks

To stalk who stalks you

And not a single blade

not a single blade

betrayed you

ODE TO THE RED RIVER CART

"an interminable shriek of grinding wood"[10]
— Joseph Howard, *Strange Empire: Louis Riel and the Métis People*

1.
Just a cart made of wood and shaganappi
pulled by a draft animal
triggered a sound that was "hellish, horrifying and nerve-wracking,"[11]

A wooden squealing wheel hub
twisting in a dry wooden axle
shattered the prairie stillness
in its continual drone
driving anything within fifteen miles out of sight
Deer and coyotes fled in opposite directions
Groundhogs dug deeper
birds lifted and scattered
to its "tooth-stabbing screech"[12]

its relentless twisting waves of squealing
bore a hole from ear to brain
a sound worm twisting, coiling
altering anyone's sense of

moving or still
big or small
near or far
straight or crooked

the Métis on their seasonal hunt walked
dazed in this ethereal wailing netherworld

of " a thousand fingernails being drawn across a thousand panes of glass."[13]

2.

This is the gratitude?

This is what's remembered after busting your knots over every boulder, rut, ditch, gopher hole from Winnipeg to St. Paul? Draggin your heavy ass through mud hole after muskeg, ooze past your spokes and weighed down by nine hundred pounds of raw buffalo-hide stuffed pemmican sausages?

This the thanks for converting to a fortress when drawn in a circle against an enemy, wheels facing outward, carts wedged together protecting everything inside it.

This is gratitude for being an all-terrain vehicle transforming into a raft to ford rivers and creeks

This, a mind-altering earworm?

Well, after all, you are just two six-foot wooden spoke wheels
dished, broad-rimmed, and shaganappi bound,
fixed to parallel, twelve-foot shafts
with a mortised wooden box
all drawn by a draft animal.

FIDDLE BIDS US

the first high call of the fiddle bids us dance
baits with its first pluck and saw of the bow
reels us, feet flick — fins to its lure and line
steady second fiddle stoking the fire below
our Red River jig and step-dance will witness
that we long kissed this earth with our feet

that we long kissed this earth with our feet
before the surveyors executed their dance
of lines and stakes at the corners to witness
the Dominion's decree to leave just fiddle and bow
and no quarter sections to bury our relatives below
because we resisted the government's line

because we resisted the government's line
we will now dance and speak with our feet
our provisional council will guide us from below
their suffering and sacrifice renewed our dance
our single-minded celebration of the fiddle and bow
will continue for generations to be our witness

will continue for generations to be our witness
when politics and greed try to twist our lines
we'll commence to jig to fiddle and bow
when the fiddler arrives we'll vote with our feet
we, the improvident ones, proclaim our dance
to the ministers and lords who tried to set us below

to the ministers and lords who tried to set us below
our well documented petitions will be our witness
when Imperial powers elect to perform their dance
the "greasy rebels" and "unhung felons"[14] will not fall in line

because the Métis forevermore will vote with their feet
now that the Dominion has left us with fiddle and bow

now that the Dominion has left us with fiddle and bow
who will call the dance, but our ancestors below
who have directed us to vote with our feet
drops of brandy and the Reel of Eight will witness
how we generated our own steps and lines
without permission from the National dance

dance bow   line below   witness feet

JUST TELL ME WHEN
THE FIDDLER ARRIVES

1st change

The fiddler rosins up his bow
we had to fly him here just for tonight

rouses our toes, servant to the teasing bow
tunes us to the strumming guitar, second fiddle
lured in the fiddler's trance
feet stitched to the fiddle strings
we step-shuffle in time

2nd change

A rising lilt lights the fiddle that fuels our feet
a little faster, the flipping sash in time with the music
heating the blood in unison with the shining fiddle
pinning us there with its reel and bounce

Breakdown

In the breakdown,
it's a duel of feet and fiddle
the fiddler sawing a flaming bow
friction of flying feet fanning its licking flames
faster, faster in an exercise that will lead to: FIRE
but the fiddlers and dancers know to put it out

He was cheap, but boy he could sure jig
he was a terrible drunk, but a fine step-dancer
you couldn't trust her, but she'd win every jigging contest

SHE WORRIES BEADS

through bead she has swelled
through thread she is held
through needle she is steadfast
pressed, grip-polished words more than once
against her sacred heart
the beads she worries through, now
are smooth black river stones
water-worried
each bead-berry clasped
to the next seed in prayer
Miyo Saint Anne —
a bead for every morning
of her thread pulling through
napew, awasis, maskihkiy
hides, needles, awls, shawls,
beads, seeds trail her
black seeds strung in rosaries
hung above her bed
in sleep she worries through them

WITH SECOND SIGHT, SHE PUSHES

sitting close to light
falling through a window
glancing down a needle
along a thread
to the centre
of a bright bead
is her belief
in petal, stem, and leaf

she directs a long thin needle
picks one tiny seed
bead, after seed
bead, after seed
from a saucer
until she has drawn a long white string with

                                        her fingers

at the end of a needle

her fingers, nudge their seeds side by side
looping their weight into a petal
laid flat against the fabric nap
each seed pressed
against the cloth by the thumb and forefinger of her left hand
while thumb and forefinger of her right
plumb the unseen side of the fabric with
another needle and thread, and
with second sight, she pushes
the needle and thread up precisely
where her eye wants to meet it
on the surface of the fabric

then down
between each bead
by seed bead
seed

over and over
repeated
this gesture petal
takes patient shape

o

the bead's colour makes no sound
but it is cranberry, moss, and fireweed
it is also wolf willow, sap, and sawdust
as well as Chickadee, Magpie, and Jackrabbit

a bead is not simply dark blue
but Saskatoon blue

it's not merely black,
but beaver head black

and it's not just a seed bead
it's a number 11 pearlized bead
or a number 10 two-cut glass bead
or a number 8 French white heart

o

the fabric weightless
supple through her lissome fingers
the waxed thread yielding
and the bright beads
obedient as good children
lining up in straight rows
inside the white outline
of a petal

but as she shifts
to light
falling on her beadwork
her thoughts turn to stem
how it attaches
to petal and leaf

slim stem
bloodline to root
and back to leaf

and she the link
like stem
from rich root
to sprouting leaf
her children

she, this link
holds
each beadberry

a thought
each beadberry
a word in prayer

for her son
for her daughter
for her grandchild

o

she considers blue beads as holding a piece of the sky
reflected in berries
her same fingers gather saskatoons draping from branches bent
    blue with fruit
and release them to the lard pail tied to her waist
their dropping, the sound of small drumming in the pail
her same fingers scoop saskatoons, the fruit of feasts
from a bowl in the sweat
that place of gathering self
and others back to womb
that bulb of life
in her mother

each bead a birth, she senses
as light grows faint as thread

each bead a birth, she sees
her eyesight fine as thread

each bead a birth, she listens
each bead sewn down, a word   in prayer

SKY BERRY AND WATER BERRY

her sisters, the flowers

her brothers, the berries

emerge from her beadwork

chokecherry red, goldenrod yellow, and juniper berry brown

sky berry and water berry

swell from her fingertips

sprout runners and cleave

to stems near the scent

of warm saskatoons

and sour gooseberries

petal, berry, stem, and leaf

sewn down now in seed bead lines

flourish bright from her hands

through her fingers stretch fields of strawberries

their starched white petals

raised heads above layers of green leaf

through tiny seed beads

she is linked

to lineage

through the inheritance of her mother's

awl case, knife sheath, and hide scraper

she is acquainted with moose and deer

their velvet smoke-tanned hide

what they have given up

what they have shared

with her, with her mother and grandmother

how they have sacrificed themselves to

sky berry

water berry

like the life-liquid of berries, her brothers

thirsted for in ceremony

and recalled now in colour

their small fruit

tasting of blossom

Beads the right size and colour

If you follow the trail of yellow seeds
fixed by her nimble fingers
in the dark velvet earth
you will surface in
the sun-swollen prairie
where buttercups blink open
coneflowers nod their heads
and dandelions ignore you completely

If you follow the trail of blue seeds
pushed into the nap of loam
by her callused fingertips
bold crocus will raise their furry heads in the raw air
bluestem will feather in front of you
and slough grass will inflict paper cuts if you yank them

And if you bend to examine a buttercup
your eye will follow the rim of its inner eye
convex and pollen-swollen
then, you will finally understand
why she searched countless beads
for the right size and colour

THE LAND SHE CAME FROM

*"If men had wings and bore black feathers, few of them would be
clever enough to be crows"*
— Reverend Henry Ward Beecher, mid-1800s[15]

cree woman crow
cree woman caw
black shiny bird-woman
crow and caw those who
command you, "Go back to the land you came from"[16]

so shiny black bird-woman plants herself
in front of Frank Oliver's house[17]
has her photograph snapped in 1885
her image singed into his pupils
into the inky black-and-white pages
of his *Bulletin*
the official but negative space
in Edmonton's story
not the other story
of Métis river lots
severed into city blocks

a quarter for a Métis river lot
crow knows what was what
when it all went wrong[18]

cree woman crow
cree woman caw
call out those names
caw caw caw: Rutherford
call out those names

names that now mysteriously bear title
to land once granted your husband
his reward for thirty years HBC service
as carpenter and blacksmith

a quarter for a halfbreed lot
crow knows what was what
when it all went wrong

cree woman crow
cree woman caw
crow and caw names
of those known as "better men"[19]
when Indians couldn't own land
call out their names
caw caw caw: Oliver
stand iron-fisted before
his two-storey-red-brick-house
rising civil in the background

a quarter for a Métis river lot
crow knows what was what
when it all went wrong

cree woman crow
cree woman caw
crow woman dig down
scrape away the layers
of sleeping memory
down to the stake lines of river lots
in Rossdale and beyond

far down to the Métis family names
still breathing there: Donald, Bird, Ward
push away the top soil, sand, and silt
to names: Daigneault, Charland, Gladue
uncover their stories of migration
to build and supply Beaver Hills House
before *it all went wrong*

uncover the names of profiteers
Lord Strathcona, for one
snapping up script and reserve land
for the price of a sack of groceries
when Papaschase's people
were starving and deprived of rations
recite his name: Papaschase, Papaschase, Papaschase
so it won't wash away in the flood of "progress"

The black mare

Every night Narcisse tried to "beat the devil." The soft sweep of
three cards in his right hand brushing the table, laid down with
a deliberate snap, measured his day as Dehlia measured hers by
the rhythmic winding of Big Ben, her thin grey braids swinging in
unison. And as Narcisse snapped his cards, she wound her clock;
neither of them paused, afraid time would slip away from them as
they slept

And they drifted,
Narcisse dream-following his nose to the dry-hay-smell of horses,
their fading hooves bidding him further away from his vow at
Lent — to give up. While Dehlia pranced, a black mare, forelock
lifting in the wind, muscled thighs, ready to spring her beyond,
Narcisse, six-and-a-half furlongs, and those two-little-hands marking
time, altogether. While Narcisse was hobbled to a fast track, the
inside post, his favourite palomino, and the sweet-sweet winning
flash of the jockey's red silks. It wasn't *his* palomino, he didn't own
anything, but he might have, if he hadn't flirted so much before.

And they flirted,
The black mare's withers flinching at the post, Narcisse edgy at
the wicket, combing a sweaty palm through his thick wavy hair. His
thoughts tumbling in digits: two-, five-, ten-dollar wagers, two-year-
old fillies, and six-and-a-half furlongs. He's still in reverie when at
the starting gun the black mare breaks first, her strides steady on
the turns, lengthening on the straightaways while his palomino's
legs, appear to be shortening and slowing. The crowd heaves in
surprise when the black mare leads on the final turn, and Narcisse,
seeing his palomino in last, crushes the ticket in his pocket and
turns away from the track, sucking his teeth.

The next morning, he wakes remorseful to the sounds of Dehlia humming as she stirs the oatmeal in the scarred kettle-of-their-years-together.

He is weak with guilt, knowing Dehlia will chastise him, chide him that all his money ever does is feed the horses, feeds them their oats and hay. He knows she'll badger him to take confession. So he says nothing.

And they twisted,
Narcisse having lost his savings during the previous night's dream, wagers with the profits from the sale of his best draft horse the second, but his palomino loses again to the black mare in the ninth race. The third night, he wagers with the money from the sale of his prized buckboard. But the same black-arse-of-a-mare trots into the Winner's Circle.

> Awake the fourth night, he hears Dehlia mumble through a
> gauze of sleep, "I can't help it."
> What? He ruminates, suspecting her of cheating.
> He's curious what else she might reveal.
> But she is silent after that.

> So when he is woken the following night by Dehlia
> mumbling, "I can't help it."
> Straight away, he asks, "What? Can't help what?"
> And with the precision of a timepiece, she chimes,
> "When I leave this house, I change into a black mare."

Narcisse is stunned. Her words reel in his head, leaving him to dangle in his thoughts. He watches her the entire night. And just as the moon is in the night-sky-highest, she leaves. He trails; her body, a draft flowing out the back door into the honey-eyed moonlight reflecting off her white flannel gown until she vanishes, dissolving into the blackness of the barn door. Narcisse follows slowly, pauses, looks back to the house, but wills himself through the darkness into the barn. Yet all he sees is the outline of his remaining horses, hears them shifting their weight in the stalls, smells the hay, oats, and horseshit. He calls her name in the moist air. There is no answer. In hopes she will reappear, he sits down on an upturned feed bucket. But he falls asleep, and when he wakes, it's morning and he finds her back in their bed, her flannel back turned out. His fingers move to brush her back, but recoil at the scent of boiled kidneys, the blood-metal scent stinging his nostrils, spawning memories of relatives bitten by Rougarous, his Mooshom warning him to smudge all used clothes for fear of being marked. Images of Dehlia moving weightless through the night in her hand-me-down nightgown fuse with his Mooshom's tales of men turning into dogs, flying horses, and crooked spines. Narcisse nervously gathers Dehlia's vials of Holy Water, her father's rosaries, and his worn deck of cards. For the first time in a long time he prays fearful they have been tricked, that they have mistakenly crossed over. He prays in Cree: Notahwenan; he prays in Michif: Li Boon Jeu; he prays English: Amen. When she wakes, she's startled seeing him surrounded by holy water, rosaries, and playing cards; she fears someone has died and he acknowledges the question in her expression.

"You've been tricked by a Rougarou," he says.
"Rougarou?" she scoffs, "Wacistakac, those horses have you charmed."
Shaking his head, "No, they've charmed you — they've hooked me."
"Hooked you?" Her face a sleepy question mark.

"Charmed you," he repeats, his words an echo.
"Charmed you."

And they recoiled,
Dehlia, never having known Narcisse to look so terrified, relents and removes the second-hand nightgown he has cautioned her about before. Narcisse bearing it like a dead bat on the end of a broom, takes it to the refuse barrel and sets it ablaze. In the light of the flame, Narcisse broods over what they must do to purge the Rougarou. He knows it will take them all night to haul and heat water, to bathe, to ready their best clothes, smudge, and pray. Not one, not two, not three times, but thirteen times they'll have to circle the house backwards in their newest clothes, backwards with an Ace of Spades pressed to Dehlia's forehead, backwards before Mooshom's time, before Narcisse, before Dehlia, winding them all backwards in time before the Rougarou.

YOU ARE RIDING
FOR THE BORDER TONIGHT

I fear that Middleton's men will track you like a deer in the woods
that a single shot will make your life   bleed berries
on the ground around you   I fear they will find your limbs
slumped in what they
think is surrender   I fear they will smile at your mouth
drooping slack-death
before them   I fear they will drag you a trophy carcass
hung from their saddle
so ride, Gabriel ride   swift-safe in the night, ride without rest
if you have to   far southward away   where I'll find you
ride swift, ride silent   rest only beyond the border
safe from the Canadiens that stalk your breath

I have little but six buckwheat cakes, wrapped warm till they reach you
as I would send my arms if I could in the chilled morning
so ride, Gabriel ride   swift-past Les Anglais' vengeance
ride swift, ride silent   ride safe

RED RIVER FRAMED HOUSES & DUST

We eat dust for days at Batoche   and think of the men, women,
and children who lived and loved this country in spite of itself
where the wind gives in to no one's prayers   not even
Manitou's   where the wind-dust blasts skin, settles like soot in our
eyes, ears, and hair   where Red River framed houses, assembled
like puzzles   are steadfast against the same devil wind   but
window- and door-less, now   yet witness to the women and
children hidden along the river's banks   the young and old
men hunkered in the deep trenches   dug against the zealous
Orangemen who hunted them   houses once witness, to the
sharpest sounds of the escalating Gatlin gun   its
rhythmic assault on the ears of six-year-old boy who smashed caste
iron for shot   houses once witness, to the life that thrived despite
all attempts by the Lords of the day to deny it   houses once
witness, to the people who drove their squeaking carts to the river
and floated across a broad-shouldered South Saskatchewan
carving through the palm of Batoche   leaning against
its knuckled-slopes grown thick with bone willow and bruised
poplar   extending a hand to the waves of wheat   in the
minefields where   the memory is deeper than the dust-bones
of those who deserved to dance forever

To a fair country

I want to forget their names, the generals"
— Rosalind Brackenbury, "Poetry in Time of War"

I want to forget their names,
the scrip commissioners and their escorts
land speculators:
bankers, members of parliament, lawyers, shopkeepers, and clergy
and how the bank and church held hands

I want to forget their hands
fast as poker players
dealing blue-green scrip coupons
stiff as new money
to northern Métis waiting for a homeland through survey
and a Land Titles office
existing only in the south

I want to forget the official trickery
the northern Métis
and their southern impersonators
redeeming land with their right hand
and conferring it with their left
into the smooth palms of speculators

I want to forget their ordinary faces
their benign smiles and dim hearts
their mundane treachery
and accumulating assets

I want to forget their orderly ledgers
lists, records

and deceptively even-handed calculations

I want to forget a travelling thirty-six-man scrip commission
with twenty-six speculators
I want to forget their numb greed and narrow vision
I want to forget their dollar-an-acre thefts

I want to forget the fraud and forgery
Crooked schemers, connivers and collaborators

I want to forget the 1921 amended Criminal Code of Canada
and its three-year time limit on scrip fraud

And finally, I want to forget the number of Métis
less than one percent
who hold property from that scrip today

WHAT'S LEFT

three pieces — white porcelain doorknob

once hardball in the palm of a hand
turned to enter a silent kitchen
steaming kettle wood cookstove stoked
on the table a drawn hand of poker: deuce of diamonds and jack of
clubs, face up

cast iron stove shards
only a memory of la galet akwa la rababoo

a horse's bit
for Gabe's prized saddle horse or buffalo runner

shards of a rusted knife
manishamihk (to cut)

a bottle stop
pour la bwaysoon ou li vaen
ga minihkwawn (I'd like a drink)

a brass weight
shiny and mercantile

a hanger
for Madeleine's capot

shell casings
from Gabe's Belgian .38 calibre Lefaucheux revolver

plate shards
wetoushpahminan (eat with us)

THE SHOWMAN & SHOW INDIANS

In the Congress — Rough Riders of the World, I am gainfully
employed as an Indian, where I parade into the big top riding
a buffalo runner, holding *Le Petit,* flanking Buffalo Bill raising
Lucretia Borgia to the cheering crowds in the bleachers, feeding
their desire to see "the principles of stereotypes and archetypes of
the West"[20] and the "breaking of fractious steeds,"[21] whirlwind races
against Mexicans, Bedouins, Gauchos, Vaqueros and Cossacks, we
ride into the arena dust carried by the sound of the Star Spangled
Banner, the press of horses, jangle of tack, the vibrating crowd
in the presence of smoked buckskin, fringes, feathers, headdress,
eagle staff, breast plate and braids, we ride under bright lights to
the boom, boom, boom of the marching band's kettle drum. Little
Sure Shot shooting a dime from Frank Butler's fingers, she with
her L.C. Smith double-barrelled hammerless shotgun, the cavalry
with Winchesters. We ride, Pahaska, the showman marshalling the
re-enactment of the Battle of Little Big Horn, a bison hunt, a train
robbery, the attack of a burning cabin, we ride whooping pageantry,
in mock battles before the Improved Order of the Red Men, we
show Indians, those of the horse and buffalo culture given a final
chance to be ourselves and many had a good time playing Indian;
the only safe kind to be

RICH IN HORSES

we had snow horses and we had saw horses — both melted
we had stuffed horses and we had stick horses — they decayed
we had skid horses and we had mules — both became obsolete
we rode saddle horses and some of us rode brocs
there were horses in our eyes but more in our heads
we had stories and bet on horses, and sometimes they became one
we had many horses but never owned one
we had bold horses and we had silent ones
we had hunters, saddle and pack horses
we rose small, swift buffalo runners
and drove lumbering Belgian skid horses
we had many horses but never owned one
we rose horses and they raised us

REQUIEM FOR LOUIS RIEL

(To the tune of "Cold, Cold Heart" by Hank Williams Sr.)

I know you tried to make men see what they would not believe

Yet many knew that you were right   and you left a legacy

And now they write about your thoughts   as if they were a crime

Why can't this nation just admit   'n' see its cold, cold part

No other man before your time   knew just what you knew then

That's why they had to do away   with what you could soon spin

And now we sing about those men   that took the life from you

Why can't this nation just admit   'n' see its cold, cold part

They'll never know just what they did   to see us sit and cry

It made us just try harder to   protect our ways of life

But now they value our beliefs   about this dying earth

Why can't these people just admit   'n' see their cold, cold part

There was a time when I believed that justice would be served

But those who needed change the most   haven't got what they deserve

And as their methods fall apart   who will they turn to then

Why can't this nation just admit   'n' see its unjust heart

Post Battle of Batoche: Gatling Gun

(Found Poem)

One Frenchman, Paul Chelet, went to the camp and upon speaking with an English officer, said to him: "Do you know how many you have killed with your Gatling gun?"

"No."

"Well, I know."

"How many? Tell me, I'd be happy to know."

"Well, you killed one."

"Ah!" cried the officer. "That's not possible."

"Yes! And it was my dog."

The officer was furious, believing that the other wanted to tease him and he was ready to hit him.[22]

OUR PRINCE

If only your fine mind could have leapt
in another time
along this colony's narrow path
to nationhood

It's not just that the path is narrow
but it's also borrowed from
another people
another place.

Be it trouble, tremble, or terror
you had to walk before the gallows
alone or with the priest
that betrayed you at Batoche
anointing your last rites

God curse them, Louis. They will regret this!

Regret hanging you

It will be the shadow side of Canada's story
indelible as the iron stakes of ancestral memory
on this grid map, witnessing clearly
how the quarter sections got divvied up at meal time
who received 200 thousand-acre grazing leases
or railway "mile belts"
who accumulated in the greasy politics of real estate
while there was still no land for the Métis

They will regret taking our prince, our prophet
And it will manifest in the marking of places

previously touched by you, Louis
the one who gave us Manitoba
brokered pluralism
and language rights

They will regret taking our prince
our prophet, the one among us gifted,
our seer
because when they look across these plains
they will see the monuments built to him
the days named after him in recognition
and when their children ask
what Louis did
they will have to answer

Louis' last vision

"Father, I see a gallows on top of that hill," said Louis,
"and I am swinging from it."

in that vision, did you see the limbs of young aspen swaying at
Batoche,
the infinity symbol flying there beside the cross
St. Antoine de Padua church with its bullet holes

from the corner of your eye did the light
flicker briefly flash of L'Assomption sash whip in the air
was it Gabriel scouting at dusk? Did you hear him call?

did your sight follow the white line of the sky
looking into eyes of Marguerite, her profile fading
your children huddled behind her

did you see the Exovedate on the Feast of St. Joseph

END NOTES

1. F.R. Scott, "Laurentian Shield."
2. Freedman, Russell. *Buffalo Hunt.* New York: Holiday House, 1988.
3. Woodcock, George. *Gabriel Dumont.* Edmonton: Hurtig Publishers, 1976, p. 425.
4. Zinovich, Jordan, *Gabriel Dumont in Paris: A Novel History.* Edmonton: University of Alberta Press, 1999, p. 61.
5. Barkwell, Lawrence. Ed. *La Lawng: Michif Peekishkwewin. The Heritage Language of the Canadian Metis. Volume 1: Language Practice.* Winnipeg: Pemmican Publications, 2004. (Wintering camps have been identified as one of the social structures under which the language Michif developed), p. 8.
6. Howard, Joseph. *Strange Empire: Louis Riel and the Metis People.* Toronto: James, Lewis & Samuel, 1952.
7. Wiebe, Rudy. *River of Stone: Fictions and Memories.* Toronto: Vintage Books Canada, 1995.
8. Howard. p. 117.
9. *Gabriel Dumont Memoirs,* edited and annotated by Denis Combet, translation by Lise Gaboury-Diallo. Saint Boniface, Manitoba: Les Editions Du Ble, 2006, p. 105.
10. Howard. p. 55.
11. Ibid. p. 56.
12. Ibid.
13. Ibid.
14. Ibid. p. 41.
15. Savage, Candace. *Bird Brains.* Vancouver: Greystone Books/Douglas & McIntyre, 1995.
16. The poem's subject, Elizabeth Brass Donald, Cree/Salteaux, was born 1836, a member of the Key Reserve signed under Treaty 4 located in southwestern Saskatchewan. At age seventeen, she married George Donald, Métis HBC carpenter and blacksmith and raised eleven children. Later she became a member of the Papaschase Band, but extinguished her Indian status by taking Métis Scrip in July 1885 likely under duress of starvation. *Edmonton Pentimento: Re-Reading History in the Case of Papaschase Cree,* Dwayne Trevor Donald.

    In two surviving photographs of Elizabeth Brass Donald (Betsy Brass), she is diminutive, with rounded shoulders, and wears a dress of crisp black fabric and a black shawl. In one photograph she stands defiant in front of Frank Oliver's house, the owner of *The*

Bulletin, Alberta's first newspaper that advocated the Papaschase Band "be sent back to the country they originally came from." R.S. Maurice, *Statement of Claim: The Papaschase Indian Band No. 136., Pimohtewin: A Native Studies E-Journal,* October 2, 2001.

17. Frank Oliver, the founder and editor of Alberta's first newspaper, *The Bulletin,* was opposed to the establishment of the Papaschase Reserve in what is now South Edmonton, and he was amongst a vociferous group of Edmontonians who adopted this attitude. They argued that the Reserve would impede the growth and development of the town and deny the settlers access to valuable resources and fertile land.

18. The line "when it all went wrong" is a derivation of "Where it went wrong." As Neil McLeod explains, "This is the English translation of the Cree word *e-mayikamikahk* which refers to the tragic events of the so-called Northwest Resistance of 1885." *Edmonton Pentimento: Re-Reading History in the Case of Papaschase Cree,* Dwayne Trevor Donald. See also Neil McLeod, "Nehiyawinwin and Modernity" in P. Douaud and B. Dawson (Eds), *Plain speaking: Essays on aboriginal peoples & the prairie* (pp. 35–53). Regina: Canadian Plains Research Centre.

19. Ibid.

20. Bird, Elizabeth, S. Buffalo Bill, and Sitting Bull. *American Indian Culture and Research Journal* 28 no. 2, 145–7. www.sscnet.ucla.edu/indian.

21. Combet, Denis, Ed. *Gabriel Dumont: Memoirs.* Trans. Lise Gaboury-Diallo. Saint-Boniface: Les Éditions du Blé, 2006.

22. Howard. p. 362.

Published by ECW Press
2120 Queen Street East, Suite 200, Toronto, Ontario, Canada M4E 1E2
416-694-3348 | info@ecwpress.com

Get the eBook Free
Purchase the print edition and receive the eBook free!
For details, go to ecwpress.com/eBook.

Library and Archives Canada Cataloguing in Publication

Dumont, Marilyn, author
    The pemmican eaters / Marilyn Dumont.

"a misFit book".
Poems.
Issued in print and electronic formats.
ISBN 978-1-77041-241-5 (pbk) ISBN 978-1-77090-721-8 (pdf)
ISBN 978-1-77090-722-5 (ePub)

    1. Riel, Louis, 1844–1885–Poetry. 2. Métis–History–Poetry. I. Title.

PS8557.U53633P44 2015   C811'.54   C2014-907629-0
C2014-907630-4

MISFIT

Editor for the press: Michael Holmes
Cover and text design: Rachel Ironstone
Cover painting: Linus Woods
Cover map image courtesy of University of Manitoba Archives & Special
Collections | Josiah Jones Bell Fonds, Maps (MSS 157): 1869-1874 (3),
Box 2, Folder 3.

Printed by Coach House Printing   5

The publication of *The Pemmican Eaters* has been generously supported by the Canada
Council for the Arts, which last year invested $157 million to bring the arts to Canadians
throughout the country. We acknowledge the support of the Ontario Arts Council
(OAC), an agency of the Government of Ontario, which last year funded 1,793
individual artists and 1,076 organizations in 232 communities across Ontario, for a
total of $52.1 million. We also acknowledge the financial support of the Government
of Canada through the Canada Book Fund for our publishing activities, and the
contribution of the Government of Ontario through the Ontario Book Publishing Tax
Credit and the Ontario Media Development Corporation.

  Canada Council   Conseil des Arts
for the Arts   du Canada

   ONTARIO ARTS COUNCIL
CONSEIL DES ARTS DE L'ONTARIO

Ontario Media Development
Corporation   an Ontario government agency
un organisme du gouvernement de l'Ontario

Printed and bound in Canada